MW01290825

Contents

Introduction

Hydroponics systems for marijuana growers have been around for a long time. Over time, numerous kinds of systems have evolved, allowing you to choose the perfect hydro system for your own lifestyle and growing preferences.

Regardless of which type of hydroponics system you decide to use, you will need to have a complete understanding of the nutrients involved in order to have a successful harvest. The type and distribution of these nutrients is different from what you would need when growing in soil. Even if you have grown marijuana in soil before, you should read this guide so that you know what you will need to do differently.

There are many different hydro system, each with it's own advantages and disadvantages. The more advanced the growing technique is (like Aeroponics) the higher the possible yield.

Here we will cover some of the details that make different systems distinctive from one another, as well as the types of nutrients you will need to provide your plants in any hydroponics system.

If you re a newcomer to the world of marijuana growing, you re probably still 100% sure that you need soil to grow your plants, right? If so, you are incorrect, because there are also hydroponic gardening systems specifically designed to grow weed without the need for soil.

Although a hydroponics growing system probably seems like something from the future, its roots lie firmly in the past. Ancient civilizations knew how to plant weed and were experimenting with hydroponics thousands of years ago. It has been suggested that the famed Hanging Gardens of Babylon were created using such systems.

Whether or not you believe that King Nebuchadnezzar II helped build the gardens in the 6th century BC or not, it does seem likely that the Aztecs used hydroponics for farming in 10th century Mexico.

In the modern era, hydroponic systems create some of the world s most fragrant and potent cannabis. Keep reading to discover how to grow marijuana indoors using the best hydroponic system for your needs.

In Latin, the word hydroponics means literally water working. Growing marijuana with hydroponics is the practice of growing plants in either a bath or flow of highly oxygenated, nutrient enriched water. Growing marijuana hydroponically simply means that you grow the plants in an inert, sterile growing medium instead of in soil. All of the plants nutrient requirements are supplied when you mix water with the nutrient solution. Hydroponics introduces the water, nutrients and air to the roots through the growing mediums and since using hydroponics bypasses the web of roots and the energy required for the plant to acquire the nutrients you get faster growing plants.

Advantages of hydroponics

Hydroponics will offer you the highest potential yield out of any method. You maximize a marijuana plants growth by growing in water. Although it might sound a bit strange for a plant to grow without soil, there are actually plenty of examples of plants that grow wild in the water.

One of the advantages of a hydroponics system is that it's much easier to control the addition of various nutrients. You ll only require enough substrate to allow the plant to remain upright.

Advantages of hydroponics marijuana

Because of the open nature of the root system in hydroponics, nutrients and oxygen also circulate easily, which further improves the efficiency of the plant. In reality, this means that certain aspects of hydroponics cultivation are easier than growing a plant in soil. It s easier to check on nutrient levels and the hydration of the plant too.

Soil has some advantages, but the yield isnt one of them, especially if you re an indoor grower.

Hydroponics offers the highest potential yields when the process is followed properly.

For a lot of growers, especially professionals, that is the be-all and end-all. That makes the decision. In addition to that high yield, Cannabis grows fastest in a hydroponics system. Plus, it s much easier to keep the environment clean and clear of parasites, insects, bacteria, or other pests.

The biggest downside is cost. Initial investment costs for hydroponics systems can be extremely high. The silver lining is that your quick turnover and high potential yields should balance out quickly over time. You also have to spend extra on auxiliary equipment: you need to be able to measure and analyze the EH, pH, and other environmental factors if you want any degree of success.

You also don t have an opportunity to get good natural flavors in your harvest when you grow with hydroponics systems.

Growing marijuana in a hydroponic system:
When you use a hydroponics system to grow your plants, you won t require any soil. Instead, you ll use another form of substrate some sort of material which has the ability to retain water and minerals, as well as allow a root system to take hold. Some of the more commonly used materials include vermiculite, coconut fiber, clay pellets, perlite, and rockwool. Below we ll talk a little bit about your different options when it comes to substrate. For complete plug & play hydroponic grow systems.

Rockwool

Rockwool is a light-weight and cheap mineral which does an excellent job of retaining water. It s made up of basalt and a silica compound. You can purchase it shredded up, as a small block, or in large 1-meter plaques.

You don t need to water rockwool very much because of how well it retains moisture. Because of this, it s important to keep tabs on how much water your plant is getting. Too much water and you risk fungus and a lack of oxygen in the roots.

Because of its affordability and efficiency, rockwool is commonly used by professionals for Cannabis cultivation. Take note, however that it does have issues, especially for amateurs or those who aren t experienced in using the material.

Growing Hydroponic with Rockwool

Be careful not to use isolation rockwool. This type can often contain chemicals that you absolutely do not want anywhere near your plant.

Make sure you are using rockwool that is meant for growing and cultivating plants, as it s a fairly versatile product. Also be careful about dry rockwool. It can irritate the skin and disintegrate into tiny pieces which can destroy the lungs. Make sure you are using some sort of breathing filter if you are working with dry rockwool. When properly moistened, this is less of an issue.

Rockwool is naturally alkaline and growers need to be sure that they neutralize it in a solution of pH 4-5 before using it as a substrate for their plants. The neutralization process can take up to a full day.

Tip: make sure to download my free Grow Bible for more information about growing hydroponic

Because of rockwool s excellent retention, you need to make sure it is getting fresh water and not building up too many minerals and impurities. Above all, don t use a platter with rockwool, and definitely don t reuse the water. This will help you prevent mold or fungal growth.

As with any substrate, hydrate your plant gradually. You don t want to suddenly drown a plant in water and nutrients that it isn t equipped to process. Read the article How To Rinse Your Growing Medium for more information

Clay pellets

Clay pellets are probably the simplest of the substrate options, even for new or inexperienced marijuana growers. They are exactly what they sound like - tiny little spheres of clay.

Hydroponic grow with clay pellets

Clay pellets dont retain a great deal of water, so they re very easy for growers to cycle water and nutrients through without worrying too much about drowning plants. The gaps between spheres are excellent channels for oxygen and nutrients to travel through, and roots prosper as a result.

Not only that, but clay pellets can be cleaned and reused ad infinitum, making them a fine choice for those looking to keep a healthy bank account.

Coconut fiber

Coconut fiber is a great natural choice for a substrate. It basically consists of the husk of the coconut, which is the substrate used by coconut seeds so that they can germinate in something which retains water and minerals, rather than sand. You ll want to make sure it s clean before you use it, but coco is naturally resistant to fungal and bacterial growth.

Coconut Hydroponics Grow

In terms of water retention, coco is not dissimiliar from rockwool. It holds a lot of water. On the other hand, it can be reused, and you don t need to worry about it causing any damage to your lungs or skin. Its sold in similar sizes and portions as rockwool. Again, make sure you aren t using a platter underneath your plant and don t reuse already drained water. As with all substrates, water gradually to avoid any risk of drowning or nutrient burn to your cannabis plant.

Perlite

Perlite is a special type of igneous amorphic stone used in agriculture, horticulture and botany as a soil amendment and also as a standalone medium for hydroponics and cuttings in early stages of growth. It resembles crumbling white pebbles.

Perlite is an excellent hydroponics substrate because it is highly permeable, but doesn t retain a lot of water. This means it will help prevent compaction and allow nutrients and water to circulate easily, which is a vital part of healthy plant growth.

Growing hydroponics in perlite

Many growers add it as an additive to other substrates. Like rockwool, you ll want to be careful when working with perlite since the tiny dust particles are dangerous to your lungs if you inhale them.

Vermiculite

Vermiculite is another natural mineral that acts sort of like an opposite to perlite. It expands with heat and retains a lot of water without being too permeable.

Vermiculite hydroponics weed

Growing in vermiculite

The main disadvantage to vermiculite is that after a long period of use, it will disintegrate and fall apart, so it needs to be mixed with other substrates for an ideal growing medium. It s commonly used in soil in ratios from between 1:5 to 1:10.

Passive systems

A passive system usually just consists of a pot or container filled with some sort of substrate, either sitting in a nutrient solution or being watered by hand. Gauze is an extremely common substrate choice in passive systems.

Passive hydroponics system weed

A pot is filled with substrate, and then strips of nylon gauze are laid in it. All of this helps the container to retain nutrient solution and then drain it and distribute it to the root systems of the plants.

Static systems

Static hydroponics are a great choice for growers looking at saving money in their grow operation. Of course, it does have disadvantages. The roots of your cannabis plant can be damaged most easily in a static hydroponics system since the water doesn t circulate well on its own.

Static hydroponics system cannabis

Static system

That means there is a higher risk of bacteria, fungus, and mold. It s not the ideal system if you are looking to grow a massive crop of plants, but it s a good starting point for growers interested in trying hydroponics systems

Open circuit systems

Open circuit hydroponics systems are very powerful and quick, but also carry a commensurate cost. These sorts of hydroponics systems require heavy fertilization, and so they also create a lot of waste.

Open circuit systems are used primarily by professional or large-scale growers. Usually, growers use coconut fiber and rockwool as substrates for open circuit systems. These types of substrates have a low permeability. They hold a lot of minerals and nutrients, so a high volume of water is required to circulate through the substrate in order to flush them out regularly.

The high water retention as well as the large amount of water that needs to be cycled through the substrate are the primary reason it s advised that amateur growers steer clear of open circuit systems. They need to be watered in meticulously measured cycles, and there isn t a lot of room for error.

The schedule and volume you need to follow when watering your substrate is dependent on the size of your Cannabis plant, the temperatures, the humidity, the levels of carbon dioxide in the environment and the substrate medium you re using.

Open circuit hydroponics system cannabis

Your roots systems will grow around pieces of substrate while an irrigation system waters the roots. Make sure any irrigation systems are properly synchronized so that you dont end up with differences in how much water is being fed to different plants or roots.

Irrigation pipes need to be installed at a slope so that water will be even distributed between plants. This is because water will flow out as quickly as it can, and plants at the end of a pipe get less water if there isn t a tilt in the pipe itself. The process of finding the right angle at which you should be tilting your pipes is a complex one.

If the process of trial and error in pipe angles is becoming overwhelming, growers can also utilize a device that will adjust the pressure at each individual dripper. Installing this sort of device will make it much simpler to evenly distribute the nutrient solution.

Keep in mind that this sort of device will also require a pump at the beginning of the irrigation system to create high pressure to begin with, otherwise the water wont move anywhere.

Again, this open circuit system isn t advised for amateur or hobbyist growers. It s a lot of work, and there is a lot of room for error.

Closed circuit system

The principles governing Cannabis cultivation in closed circuit hydroponics systems are fairly similar. Plants are irrigated with a nutrient solution, which circulates through the roots and is then gathered in a trough.

Closed circuit hydroponics system weed

This method causes significantly less waste than an open circuit system. Usually, closed circuit hydroponics systems use Perlite or clay pellets as the most common substrates. This is a great cultivation system for growers who don t want to waste a lot of nutrients, being simultaneously economically and ecologically sound.

Ebb and flood systems

The ebb and flood system is another option for hydroponics enthusiasts. The ebb and flood system functions with simple parts. To do it, you ll need a table at least 10cm deep, a nutrient solution reservoir, a pump, and a sheet of opaque plastic to protect the roots from light.

Ebb flood hydroponics system weed

You just temporarily flood the root systems of your plant with nutrient solution, then let it drain back into the reservoir. Most growers have all of this attached to an automated system which floods the roots at regular intervals.

You ll also want to make sure you have an overflow pipe set up in case something gets clogged. Your pump will fill up the table with a nutrient solution until it reaches the overflow level, then it will drain back out after giving the roots enough time to absorb it. The most complicated part of this system is figuring out how long to wait between flooding and draining.

Nutrient film technique

The nutrient film technique is a type of active hydroponic system where a solution of nutrients is drained onto a tray to create a shallow high-surface-area film that flows along through the roots of the plants.

This solution provides the plants with everything they need to grow and thrive. The roots will grow down into the tray and form a mat, taking advantage of the high surface area to maximize efficiency.

Abundant and constant availability of water and nutrients means huge yields, as long as the grower is careful to also provide plenty of oxygen and light as needed for the plant.

Nutrient film hydroponics system cannabis

It is one of the most common hydroponic system used today by commercial growers. As for home growers, there is one system, in particular, which has stood the test of time, the Gro-Tank.

The nutrient film technique was one of the first active hydroponics systems created specifically to meet the needs of growers operating out of their home. It was developed in the UK in the late 1970s and is still in use today. Assembly and operation are extremely simple, and the whole setup is very compact.

This means growers with limited space will still have plenty of room for lights and fans and all of the other space-gobbling accessories they might need to make their cultivation operation a success. From an organizational standpoint, it also works well the water reservoir is located below the system itself, so there s less danger of leakage from pressure differentials.

Growing Marijuana NFT

A different type of nutrient film technique involves a solution that is circulated through clay pellets inside of a pot that has small holes in its bottom. The solution flows out of the holes and back into the system, creating a closed loop. This setup requires a small pneumatic pump and is preferred over a traditional NFT because the uneven texture of the clay pellets force oxygen into the water.

It also is an improvement over the old version because the clay pellets enlarge the surface area and help retain water more effectively. This way, if the pumps stop working, the marijuana plants are more likely to survive.

Aeroponics systems

Aeroponics make a very impressive cultivation system. This particular method functions without substrate and grows plants by suspending roots in the air and misting them periodically with nutrient solution. A tray separates the root system from the upper part of the plant.

Aeroponics system weed

The aeroponics method lets roots absorb massive quantities of nutrients and minerals, and the plant can grow extremely quickly, producing gargantuan yields. Remember that this is likely one of the most complicated methods of growing, and you re better off gaining experience with some of the simpler methods before moving onto aeroponics.

The roots are very vulnerable in this system because they are bare. If the pump stops, plants can die extremely quickly since there is no water retention at all.

Hydroponics Nutrients

Nutrients are the foundation of all plant growth, and certainly they are one of the most important elements in successful Cannabis cultivation. In a hydroponics system, plants get all the nutrients they need from water.

That means you ll need to keep your nutrient solution well-stocked with every type of required nutrient: oxygen, potassium, phosphorus, and nitrogen. You ll want an even temperature near 68 degrees (20 Celsius)

If you decide to buy fertilizer, make sure it s suited to use in a hydroponics system and that it has all of the necessary ingredients. Chelate fertilizers are the ideal choice, they are most reliably absorbed.

Hydroponics nutrients weed

Many growers advise using a mix of different fertilizers, or even better, mixing your own fertilizer that contains just what your plants needs to reach their optimum growth. After you ve made a nutrient solution, you ll want to carefully check the concentration of the fertilizer regularly since the different levels of nutrients have a tendency to fluctuate.

Also be careful to keep an eye on the pH value of your water, since Cannabis can absorb things from the water and create unexpected reactions. Buy the best hydro nutrients at this links

pH and EC

The pH scale ranges from 0-14, with zero being the most acidic (positively charged) and fourteen being the most basic/alkaline (negatively charged). 7 is neutral. You ll want the environment your marijuana plant is growing in to be stable at between 5-6, depending on the phase of growth its going through.

Check in regularly: it can be difficult to monitor pH levels since each element of a nutrient solution has a different pH and the mixture might not be 100% homogenous.

A cannabis plant thats been grown in a hydroponics system absorbs nutrients most efficiently if the pH value of the solution is very close to 5.2. If the pH changes too drastically from this level, your plant can experience a wide array of issues, and may stop growing entirely.

pH and EC scheme

Checking pH levels is fairly simple. You can either use an electronic or chemical method of testing. Electronic testing is accurate but tends to be significantly more expensive. If you have a large growing operation, you re probably going to want the electronic tester.

If you haven t invested too much into your hydroponics system and you don t feel like measuring too often, you ll be fine with the chemical test. If your pH rises too high, you can add some acid to balance it out, and tap water should correct a low pH. Ideally, you want to mix alimentary and phosphoric acid, which works well for both growth and flowering periods of your plant.

Measure pH level

When you measure the pH level of your environment, you are measuring the electrical charge, that is, the ratio of positive or negative ions present. In much the same way, you can also measure the electric conductance, which tells you about the amount of minerals present in the solution you are measuring. Obviously the presence of these minerals is very important. Water is an excellent conductor of electricity in part because of the minerals it contains. The more fertilizers, nutrients, or minerals added to water, the better a conductor it will become.

Just as with the pH, your best bet for measuring electric conductance is an electronic device. The same is true for many other statistics, such as total dissolved solids (TDS), conductivity factor (CF) and parts per million of specific elements (ppm).

EC scheme

When your Cannabis plant is in its initial growth period, it will require a solution with an EC measuring 0.8-1.0, while during flowering the EC should be somewhere between 1.2-2.

If your EC levels rise too high in an active closed circuit system, it probably means that your plants are absorbing too much water, and not absorbing the nutrients. You can lower EC by adding additional water. If EC levels drop too low, it probably means you need to add more nutrients.

Be careful to keep a close eye on all of these measurements, because it determines the overall health and productivity of your plant. Small shifts are unavoidable and normal, but you don t want the fluctuations to be too large, or for levels to hover too low or high for too long. That will always negatively influence the health of your plant.

If you don t intend to check the levels regularly, make sure you regularly refresh your nutrient solution so you can at least approximate the right levels for what your plant needs

Nutrients 101

Marijuana plants, and in fact all plants, do not need to be in a living soil, they require nitrogen (N), phosphorus (P), potassium (K), calcium (Ca), magnesium (Mg) and sulfur (S). Those are the macroelements (the big ones) and the small elements known as microelements are iron (Fe), chlorine (Cl), manganese (Mn), boron (B), zinc (Zn), copper (Cu) and molybdenum (Mo). Growing marijuana indoors with hydroponics, water is enriched with these very same nutrient salts, creating a hydroponic nutrient solution which is perfectly balanced. An all purpose hydroponic nutrient solution with secondary elements like calcium, sulphur and magnesium and trace elements boron, copper, molybdenum, zinc, iron, and manganese will get you through all stages of growth. But depending on the stage of growth, you can adjust different nutrient levels needed at different times to optimize your yield. A 15-15-15 solution contains 15% Nitrogen; 15% Phosphorus; 15% Potassium. A 20-10-5 solution contains 20% Nitrogen; 10% Phosphorus; 5% Potassium. The percentage of the solution not used by N-P-K is trace elements and inert material. If you are buying hydroponic nutrients, get the powder kind that mixes with water. It is much cheaper over the long run when compared to pre-mixed solutions.

Conclusion

The hydroponic systems are maybe the best systems for indoor growing of marijuana. They are not that complicated to use and some of the systems are so easy to use even the complete amateurs can set them up and grow some high-quality weed.

Yes, some of the systems require more money but the results are totally worth it. Most important thing here is dedication. You can t just set up the system and come back to see it in two weeks. You have to visit the grow room daily. You need to make sure everything is ok. You need to provide the perfect conditions at all times. And most important of all you need to love your plants.

With so many different strains, you have so many choices. Maybe the first strain you pick won t be your favorite, but you will most certainly like it. It s the weed after all. But after some time, you will be more experienced and you will find your favorite strain.

It might happen that you don t do everything properly on your first try, but don t be discouraged. Never give up because the reward is pure awesomeness. You will never enjoy the weed as much as you will enjoy the one you grew by yourself.

Also, always make sure that you stay safe from the police and try not to be suspicious. We all know that weed is just a harmless plant that has many medicinal effects and that nothing bad will happen if you smoke it, but the law doesn t agree with as for now. Until they make the weed legal everywhere, stay safe and hidden from the eyes of the law enforcement.

All of my knowledge gathered here comes from the books that I mentioned in the beginning of the text and my personal experience. I also recommended a few of the alternative methods that I tried so you can choose the most suitable one for you

- N = Nitrogen
- P = Phosphorus
- K = Potassium

Higher amounts of N are needed when the temperature will be below 80 degrees in the grow room during vegetative growth. 20-20-20, or 23-19-17, or 12-6-6, or something similar, with trace elements should do it.

If temperatures are higher than 80 degrees in the grow room, you need not worry about more N in the formula during vegetative growth.

During flowering the plant needs lots of P, regardless of temperature. 15-30-15, or 5-20-10, or 2-4-3, or something similar, with trace elements should do it.

Do not over fertilize your plants as too much fertilizer will kill your plants. If you under fertilize, plants will take longer to grow but will not die. Follow the mixing instructions on your hydroponic solution package, if you aren t sure, use less rather than more.

As water evaporates it is absorbed by the plants, your water reservoir level will drop. Add tap water that has been aged 3 days or longer to the reservoir. I don t add nutrient solution when I top up the tank, some people do.

Change the nutrient solution every 2 weeks. That is, discard the old solution and clean out the reservoir, pumps, and other equipment that is used with HOT WATER. After cleaning, add tap water that has been aged 3 days or longer to the reservoir then add nutrient solution. You only need to clean the cups and tubing the plants are in before you start a new crop. More detail on nutrients.

Marijuana nutrient cycle

The timer that starts to pump the nutrient solution should turn on and the solution should submerge the plants roots about every twenty minutes. As soon as the roots are submerged, the pump can shut down. If it takes longer than 20 minutes for the roots to get water, the roots will usually grow long, and they can grow very long looking for the nutrient solution source. In fact they can grow so long and thick that they prevent the solution from reaching all the way up your grow cups. This will also raise the chance of root material being ripped out and clogging the system. Once the flow is clogged by root or other material inside, you will have to take the garden apart and clean it.

Check the root length every few weeks. If it is hard to remove the cups the plants are in because the roots are anchored to the internal channel, the roots are too long. The root should be short enough to not touch the narrow point where the solution enters the cup holder. If they are too long, trim them down with scissors. Make sure they are not going too far, but don t cut unnecessarily.   The old solution that you are discarding can be used to water house or garden plants. This will at least double the growth rate if you usually water your plants with regular tap water! More detail on nutrients.

Why not soil

In soil, biological decomposition breaks down organic matter into the basic nutrient nitrogen, phosphorus and potassium salts that plants feed on. Water dissolves these salts and allows uptake by the roots. For a plant to receive a well balanced diet, everything in the soil must be in perfect balance. Rarely, if ever, can you find such ideal conditions in soil due to the lack of organic matter left behind on the surface, contamination and biological imbalances.

Soil is not able to produce a high volume of nutrients as hydroponics can deliver. Hydroponics takes the desired amount of food directly to the root rather than making plant s roots look for it. Soil loses its nutritional value and is difficult to measure in terms of pH and fertility. With hydroponics the pH and nutritional value of the water are easily measured and maintained, so plants always have enough to eat. Only when you water your soil plants, the basic elements can dissolve into the water. In a hydroponic system, moisture is present for extended periods of time or for all the time. In addition, soil plays host to many nasty little creatures, pests and diseases while hydroponic growing mediums are inert and sterile making a very hygienic environment for the plant and owner.

Hydroponic marijuana set ups

All growing described on this page is done using the Ebb and Flow system. The Ebb and Flow system is one of, if not the most popular hydroponic methods for growing weed. It is simple and easy to use. It works like this: A reservoir containing nutrient solution is located below a growing tray. To support the plants in a hydroponic system, an inert soil-free medium like fiber or stone, may be used to anchor the roots. These hydroponic mediums are designed to be very porous for excellent retention of air and water that s necessary for a healthy plant   roots need to breathe too. The tray contains the plants in containers with a growing medium like Rockwool, lava rocks or the like. A basic system known as Ebb and Flow requires the the growing bed to be filled with a nutrient solution by a small pump on a timer to feed and water the plants, the nutrient solution flows in. The timer then shuts the pump off and the nutrient solution drains or ebbs freely back into the reservoir. Ebb and Flow systems   are favored because of their low maintenance, high productivity, and ease of use. Ideal not only for the beginner, but for the advanced gardener as well.

HTML Map

There are lots of other systems to consider:

- Aeroponics- This method of hydroponics goes without a growing medium, although a small amount may be used to germinate the seed or root a cutting. Plant roots are suspended mid-air inside a chamber kept at a 100% humidity level and fed with a fine spray of nutrient solution. This mid-air feeding allows the roots to absorb much needed oxygen, thereby increasing metabolism and rate of growth reportedly up to 10 times of that in soil and there is nearly no water loss due to evaporation. The mist is created by special nozzles to the root system on a regular basis. The roots are held inside a water proof and light proof container which helps create a high humidity area.

- Continuous flow / Top feed system - This is the system you often see pictures of. Using a 23 or 43 PVC tube with holes cut into the top at regular intervals for the plants to sit in a holder or pot. The nutrients are continuously fed down the PVC pipe over the root system.

- Deep Water Culture (DWC) + Recirculating direct water culture systems (also known as RDWC) + BubblePonics This is a simple yet effective way to grow, it is similar to the mist Aeroponics system in some ways. However the concept is to submerge the plants roots in the nutrient system, now without air they would die, so you add an air rock like used fish tanks. If you pump significant air through the system the bubbles maintain oxygen to the roots and they grow really well.

- Drip Irrigation - A great way to save water and nutes. Used throughout large outdoor farming systems to cut down on waste, small droppers are placed right next to the stem or roots of the marijuana in their pots within the medium. Small drops of the nutrient system will drip out regularly to feed the plant. Very low evaporation and good for stealth grows too because it is silent.
- Ebb and Flow- As discussed above the nutrient solution floods a tray situated above the reservoir and then ebbs back into the reservoir

in the process feeding the plants with their roots situated to the tray.

- Nutrient Film Technique (NFT)- Similar to the Ebb and Flow technique but it is more circular. The tray above the reservoir is tilted and the nutrients fed in from the top and let to drain in a thin film down the tray back into the reservoir, it lets roots feed and have access to air.

- Wick system- An easy system where by your marijuana is usually situated in pots, which can have a soil medium, there are thick wicks usually of cotton that connect the pots aggregate with their roots with the reservoir below. The nutrients solution is constantly sucked up by the plants when they are dry through capillary action.

- Sea of Green (SoG)- This is Dutch method for growing rather than a hydroponic method.
- Screen of Green (Screen of Green)- Very similar tot he Sea of Green system but involves a

screen situated above the marijuana heads, read more above Sea of Green.

Sea of Green (SOG) and Screen of Green SCOG   These growing systems are used more by commercial operations where speed and yields are paramount but can be used in smaller home grows. The equipment is different and you need cannabis strains that are capable of flowering after a short vegetation period, read more. If you would rather buy a ready built grow room rather than grab all the gear from the hardware store (they will know what you are making), it may cost a little more but all parts will be included and you will save time by getting everything at once. More about hydroponic grow systems.

Marijuana lighting

Since modern hydroponics began people have used high intensity discharge (HID) lights including Metal Halide (MH) or High Pressure Sodium (HPS) to grow marijuana and more recently with great success, LED grow lights. Metal halide light is close to regular room light or compact fluorescent light CFL and is more abundant in the blue and green spectrum s which is best for vegetative growth. While high pressure sodium HPS offer light in the orange, amber and red end of the spectrum which is best for flowering stage (later) growth. Growers often use these two lights in tandem, MH for vegging and HPS for flowering or both at the same time. Marijuana grows well from 420 through 730 nanometres which can be covered in this method. HID lamps like the MH and HPS offer a lot of light but just as much wasted energy is emitted as heat. You will need to manage that heat with a good ventilation system. HIDs also require a ballast to operate so make sure you buy one of them. Expect to pay about $250 for a 600W HPS/MH digital ballast, bulb and reflector combo.

Full spectrum LED grow lights are what the pros have turned too now, we know some of the large greenhouses (think big name seed companies) in the Netherlands have turned too as they offer far more control, lower electricity costs while heat and space issues are decreased. Why are LEDs now a good option? The cost of LEDs, their power and the color they produce (spectrum) is tuned perfectly for marijuana growing. LED grow lights, in particular full spectrum LED grow lights, number of advantages over HIDs such as covering the full grow spectrum from seedling, vegetative and flowering stages, run on approximately half the electricity and have bulb lives of around 50,000 to 60,000 hours! A 1000W HPS is the equivalent to approximately 500W LED (true draw). Good LEDs run cool, have no fans or excellent silent fans and emit very little heat   and do not require a ballast. LED grow lights are a great solution to the old HIDs. Much more on grow lighting.

Marijuana growing seeds or clones

If you know someone who grows, ask them for a few clones. If you don t have access to clones you will have to buy marijuana seeds. If you don t already have some, you can ask you friends to save you seeds out of any good weed they may come across. If you need seeds we totally recommend reading this cannabis seeds guide

Germinate the marijuana seeds

Set up your hydroponic garden before you germinate the seeds. Make sure everything works fine. If you are using clones, skip this section. There are various types of media available to grow in. Rockwool is one, but there are many others. Media simply means the substance that the roots grow in. Since you aren t using soil in a hydroponic garden, you need a substitute. The media will provide no nutrition; it is just a support for the roots. All nutrition comes from the hydroponic solution. The standard thing to do is use a Rockwool cube to start the seed on and surround it with whatever growing media you like to use. Keep the Rockwool cube so that the bottom 70% or so is submerged when the water is at its maximum, but keep the top part above the water so that the seed is never submerged. After the seeds have germinated and the root is about a quarter of an inch long, place the seed, root down, on your grow cube or media in your hydroponic cups.

Expandable grow tent options, check out The Grow Rack.

- Dorm Grow LED   High Times Winner
- Buy herbies Feminised Seeds
- Buy autofloweringseeds   Worldwide Delivery
- Buy cannabis Seeds   Worldwide Stealth
- Buy Bonzaseeds Seeds

Vegetative marijuana growth

The first phase of marijuana growth is called the vegetative phase. If you plan on using LED, MH or HPS right away, Start with about 20 inches or more above the top of the plant (less for LEDs) and lower the light an inch or so daily until you think the height is right. Too close and the plants will dry and turn brown. Too far and the plants grow too tall as they stretch to get closer to their light source. That is a waste of space. Start high and lower the light an inch or two daily until you think the height is right and the light emitted is being caught well by the plants. During the first stage of growth, the vegetative stage, keep the light on 18 to 24 hours a day minimum. The longer it is on, the faster the plants will grow, but the higher your electricity bill will be. More on marijuana vegetative growth. More on marijuana vegetative growth.

Marijuana flowering

Flowering is the phase of marijuana growth that produces the most THC, CBN and CBD; these are the active ingredients that produce a high when the female buds are smoked. Once flowering begins, the height of the plants will taper off as the plant energy is used in the flowering process itself. You can start flowering when the plants are a minimum of about 6 inches high and have at least 4 sets of leaves. This will take 2 weeks to a month of vegetative growth in most hydroponic gardens. When you want to start flowering cut the light back to 12 hours a day. If you start the flowering when the plant is very small say 6 inches the height of the plant will continue to increase for about two to four weeks after flowering has been started, after that all the plants energy will be used for flower production. If you start the flowering when the plant is a bit more mature it will start in around 10 days. Limiting the height of a marijuana plant has always been a difficult task, so one easy method is to raise the height of the light as the plant grows. There are methods of limiting the height of a plant, but none of them are really easy. We recommend one of the Marijuana Growers Guide which has the most comprehensive descriptions I have seen on limiting the height of weed. The flowering cycle lasts about two months, sometimes a little longer, depending on the type of seed. So the total length of time to raise a crop should be 3 to 4 months in a hydroponic garden but much less if you use the Sea of Green or Screen of Green methods. During flowering the dark period must be perfectly dark. No room light, sun light, or any other light should reach the plant in the 12 hours of darkness that the plant must get everyday. The strongest light that should reach the plant during flowering would equal that of moonlight. Stronger light than this will delay flowering, and if it continues there is a chance that the plant will not flower, but stay in the vegetative phase. You will know the plants are flowering when you see what look like little white hairs developing at bud sites. They should be visible after about 10 to 14 days of the flowering light cycle. This is when you need to remove the male plants, not required if you have female clones. These pistils will eventually be the red or white hairs that you see turn into nice big buds. More about marijuana flowering and sexing.

Harvesting, curing and storing marijuana   no smell

We have a great page all about harvesting your marijuana! If your weed is going to be stored for more than a year it should be wrapped in an air tight container and be stored somewhere that is dark and cool. A freezer is best, but a fridge, basement, closet, or something similar will do. Dry it first if you grow your own, or if the stuff you have is very moist. And remember that light, air and heat are the things to avoid. If you are looking to grow and smoke marijuana of course this will produce odors. Sometimes they can be strong enough to attract attention. If you would like to eliminate the smell from growing and/or smoking marijuana the best thing to do is build an ozone generator. More detail on odour control.

Tips to growing hydroponics marijuana

The cliché, an ounce of prevention equals a pound of cure may well be overused, but it is still a good measure to use when growing marijuana. If enough attention to detail is taken during the setup phase of a hydroponic grow operation, then the chances for a successful crop are greatly increased.

The precise course of action taken will depend on your unique space and resources, and of course any unique needs of the particular strain of cannabis that you are growing. All that aside, there are still some tasks and practices that should be observed in any hydroponic growing area to keep your plants as healthy and productive as possible.

- Start with sterile tanks and equipment- If you can afford to buy all new equipment to start your growing operations, this step may not be necessary at first, but eventually all tanks, reservoirs, pipes, filters and any other physical part of your hydro system will need to be sanitized to prevent the development and spread of pathogens, especially root rots. Plan on having several bottles of isopropyl alcohol and hydrogen peroxide on hand to disinfect your equipment on a regular basis.

- Make sure you start with clean, pH neutral water- Ideally the water circulating through your hydroponic system is at a pH of 7. If not, a reverse osmosis (RO) system will create and provide neutral water. Distilled water can be used as well until an RO system can be obtained.

- Watch your temperatures- Ideally the water flowing through your system will be about 65 F (18 C) to facilitate good nutrient absorption and to prevent the buildup of algae. The air temperature, however can be warmer. If you can achieve about 75 F (24 C) in your grow room, your marijuana plants should be quite content.

- Maintain proper humidity levels- Cannabis plants do best in varying levels of humidity based on their stage of development. When your girls are young, they need to have humidity levels in the 60-70 percent range. As they develop and move into the blooming phase, they only need about 40 percent humidity. This can be best achieved with a humidifier and dehumidifier used accordingly.

- Attain proper lighting- There are numerous types of grow lights out there and champions and critics of all. The right types of grow light for your setup will depend on your space, the distance between your lights and your plants and your budget. High Intensity Discharge (HID) lights are better for larger grow rooms with good airflow and ventilation. Compact Fluorescent lights (CFL) are better for smaller rooms. Light from Light Emitting Diode (LED) fixtures is good for small grow areas, but is more costly than the CFLs. Whichever type is selected, make sure that it can produce light in sufficient amounts between 400 and 700 nanometers. A relatively inexpensive light meter can help to determine if your grow lights are getting the job done.

- Maintain proper ventilation/air flow- Keeping the air moving around is critical for plant health and aids in even temperature distribution. Fans should be mounted or placed so that they can cover the most area unobstructed. Proper ventilation will help to maintain appropriate air temperatures if it gets too hot, but will also help with air exchange.

- Understand pH- Fortunately this is not difficult and there are meters that can take pH readings. This is important because if the pH of your water is not in the proper range, your plants will not grow well or may even die. For hydroponic cannabis, aim for a pH of about 6.0, but allow for a range between high 5s and low 6s.

- Understand EC readings- Electrical conductivity (EC) is a measure of the total dissolved solids (TDS) in your hydroponic water. Like with pH, there are many effective meters on the market and there are many that take both readings (pH and EC). The EC level will tell you how rich in nutrients your circulating water is. If the EC is too low, your plants aren t getting enough; if it s too high, you can burn your plants with too high of a nutrient level. The EC for hydroponically grown cannabis will fluctuate depending on the stage of growth. As seedlings or clones are first put into a system, the EC levels should be less than 1.3 and can be as low as .5 for clones. When they start to grow however, expect to maintain an EC level that continually climbs toward 2.0. When your plants finally reach the flowering phase, they may need an EC up to almost 2.5 depending on the strain grown. Check your EC levels often.

The closer you can maintain proper EC, the more productive your cannabis plants will be.

- Find a reliable seed source- All of the planning, preparation and procuring of necessary products can t make cannabis of poor genetics into a robust strain. A cannabis plant can only produce what it is genetically predisposed to produce. Improving its growing environment and attending to its needs ensures that it will come as close to this potential as possible.

- Keep good records - You cannot improve what you cannot measure. Even the best growers have bad crops and sometimes novices get lucky. To remove as much of the luck factor and to focus on results, keep track of everything. The more detailed notes you keep on temperatures, planting dates, EC levels, pH levels, humidity levels and any other factor that you can measure, will allow you to make informed decisions going forward to make continual improvements or to maintain high yields.

Made in United States
Troutdale, OR
05/08/2024

19728260R00030